I0164524

The Rebirth of

NAZISM

Ron Berger

Published by:
berger publishing
Manteca, CA 95336
authorpublisher@gmail.com

Berger Books

© 2017

berger publishing

Benefits from a Book

Printed in the USA
ISBN 13 - 978-0-9906094-5-2
First Printing
Library of Congress Control Number:
2017908669

2017

CONTENTS
Note - italicized paragraphs curtesy of

Google

Prolog   4

History Repeating Itself   19

New World Order   23

The Clintons   31

The Man with the
      Golden Tongue   39

The Nazi Ideology   42

Todays Nazis   52

Nazi Traits   61

ISIS   69

People you may know
      and love   85

Fake News   127

Reflecting   129

Epilogue   133

Finally - Again   138

Key dates in the early Nazi Party

1919: Adolf Hitler joins the German Workers Party (led by Anton Drexler). Drexler places Hitler in charge of propaganda and political ideas.

1920: Party renames itself the National Socialist German Workers Party (Nazis) and releases 25 Point Plan

Prolog

Since its adoption by the Nazi Party of Adolf Hitler, the swastika has been associated with Nazism, fascism, racism in its (white supremacy) form, the Axis powers in World War II, and the Holocaust in much of the West. The swastika remains a core symbol of Neo-Nazi groups.

"... if fascism ever comes to America, it will come in the name of liberalism."
Ronald Reagan - 1975

In the 1920's no one took a second look at Adolf Hitler. He was just another "rabble-rouser" that was really taken back because Germany lost the First World War. He needed some one to blame and a platform to announce it from. He found both in the *German Worker's Party* which became the *National Socialist German Workers Party - or NAZIS.*

He was a charismatic and powerful speaker. He never realized he had that power until he was recognized by Anton Drexler, who was then the leader of the Worker's Party. He was able to convince most who heard him that Germany allowed the Jews to make the loss of the war happen. He professed that he would be able to turn things around and all they had to do was follow him.

The middle 20's weren't good for Adolf. He and his band of misfits tried to take over the government by force, but it only landed him in jail. He handled his own defense and convinced the judge that his thinking was right for Germany, but he had still broken the law. His sentence was only one year and he could have been shot, but the judge believed he was right and really let him off the hook.

During this time he wrote his book " *Mein Kampf*" (my struggle). Hitler never actually sat down and pecked at a typewriter or wrote longhand, but instead dictated it to Rudolf Hess while pacing around his prison cell in 1923-24 and later at an inn at Berchtesgaden.

The book was never on the best seller's list until the early part of the 30's when he became Führer. It was and is basically hundred's of pages talking about his philosophies, especially about the Jews and the *superior* aryan race.

"Lebensraum", was the word for living space that Hitler talked about and the Allies never listened to. He said the German people needed more living space and that those people being displaced would appreciate it because

of the advantages that would be gained from the superior aryan race.

The German people seemed to be doing quite well and didn't listen to all of Adolf's speeches and his Nazi Party slowly lost believers. Hitler was just another loud mouth to many and paid him little attention.

After his prison stay, he realized that trying to take over the government by force wasn't getting him anywhere and was just infuriating the voting public. His next move would be to figure out a way to become a politician. He didn't have to wait too long. The stock market crash of 1929 sent Germany into a tailspin. Soup lines sprung up to handle the unemployed and he began to, again, blame the government for not doing enough for the workers. Now it was much easier to gain listeners and Nazi joiners.

Now - instead of acting like a "thug" group, the Nazi's pretended to be in sympathy with the workers. He was acting like a "savior" to the working class.

Although his tactics were working, they weren't working as fast as Adolf wished. His party was gaining seats in the Reichstag, but something else needed to be done. Fire broke out and the Reichstag went up in flames. Adolf blamed the communists and the Weimar government. Now the people really started to listen. It was never proven that Hitler initiated the fire, but the person they caught couldn't have possible made that big a fire all by himself. Besides he was a communist and a good person to hang the entire fire on him.

The Hitler Cabinet de jure formed the government of Nazi Germany between 30 January 1933 and 30 April 1945 upon the appointment of Adolf Hitler as

Chancellor of the German Reich by president Paul von Hindenburg – contrived by the national conservative politician Franz von Papen, who reserved the office of the Vice-Chancellor for himself. Originally a coalition of Hitler's Nazi Party and the national conservative German National People's Party, it became an exclusively Nazi cabinet when the DNVP was intimidated into dissolving itself.

When Hindenburg died, Hitler took full control of the government and titled himself as the Führer. This is when he repealed all the freedoms that the people had and stated that the government was now in charge and he was in charge of the government.

The people didn't seem to mind that since he promised them all a rose garden. He was actually good for the country and was able to garner very large crowds whenever he spoke. During the early years of his reign the country prospered. If he would have stopped there he would have gone down in history as the real savior of Germany instead of the most hated man in history that he became.

Now that he had sufficiently brainwashed the public, he set about his real reason he wanted to accomplish. Getting even for Germany's defeat in WW1 and the Jews, ostentatiously, for making it happen. The people looked the other way because Hitler must be right since he has done so many good things.

Once he felt that he had tweaked their minds enough, he started to do his dirty deeds. One of the most memorable was the "night of the long knives" where he personally led his troops to arrest and kill Ernst Röhm and many of the "Brown Shirt" leaders. All done, of course, in the name of keeping the country safe from "traitors".

He also stepped up his hatred of the Jews and anyone who, he thought, might want his job. Keeping this as quiet as possible so the public just wouldn't believe it to be true. He even hosted a tea party the day after the long knives night was over. Nothing ever seemed traceable back to him.

Along with making the German people feel safe and comfortable with all their good fortune, he quietly increased the military production contrary to the Versailles Treaty. At this point Adolf could do no wrong. They fell for his propaganda hook line and sinker.

The German people, in mass, didn't want another war and believed that everything Hitler was doing was in that vein. Even when he took over the Rhineland, Austria and Czechoslovakia without a shot being fired, the people praised him. It wasn't war. It was just solidifying German interests. Adolf's prestige couldn't have gone much higher.

Of course, when he invaded Poland everything started to come unglued. England and France declared war on Germany and the people got exactly what they didn't want. But, they didn't say much when Hitler did the winning in just six weeks. The people, again, shouted triumphantly and Hitler was, again, in the cat birds seat.

But now, with England and France fighting and England starting to retaliate the people started to see World War 1 all over again. They still felt Adolf knew what he was doing since he already had a great record and they were sure it would be over quickly.

However, such was not the case. Then once the Nazis invaded Russia, the people, as well as most of his generals were leery of his mental capabilities.

The Messiah of Germany was now being brought into questioning and the people found out that it was to late to do anything about it. Adolf even put the Vatican and the Catholic Church on his list of future conquests. There just wouldn't be room enough for two Messiahs. Little is mentioned in history that his invasion of Poland required the killing of as many Catholic Priests as possible.

The rest of the story is history. In the next five years, the USA and most of the world entered the war and millions of lives were lost. Although we hear a lot about the 6 million Jews that were exterminated actually about 8 - 50 million lost their lives due to Hitler's end of the war. Russia lost 20 million according to estimates. Many of those were actually done by Stalin himself.

The killing really heated up when they invaded Russia. Specially trained SS groups would follow the fighting and start eliminating the Jews and anyone else that would be considered a threat to Nazi rule.

They realized that the process was taking to long and they gathered in a special meeting for the "final solution" to the Jewish problem.

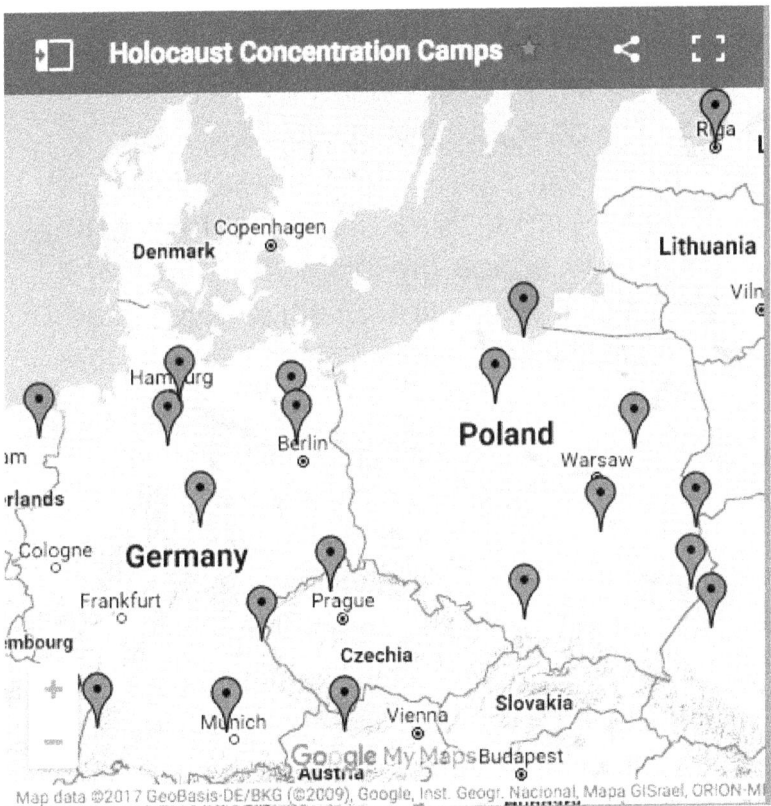

Soon concentration camps sprung up all over Poland and eventually into Germany. These were the answer to the "final solution" and very few lived to tell about it. Large factories also located next to some of the later ones so they could benefit from the free slave labor.

The sickness that Hitler instilled into his troops is unimaginable. Even they had trouble doing all that killing.

There are only a few people who occupied space on this earth that were more evil then Hitler, Stalin & Mao. Mao actually killed more people than the other two combined.

To us, killing one person is terrible, but killing millions is beyond reason. Nothing could possibly be a reason for killing so many people. Pure evil, hatred, loathing, detestation, dislike, distaste, abhorrence, abomination, execration, aversion; hostility, enmity, animosity, antipathy, revulsion, disgust, contempt, etc., Adolf had them all. Nothing but the Aryan race was good enough to rule the world. All others must be forced into submission or die. Sound familiar?

NAZI BREEDING

In order to create his master race, he needed to be able to start when they are very young. Actually the women were encouraged to have children with or without their husbands (as long as the father was pure Aryan) and as soon as possible the state would take the baby and raise it. They were wards of the state for the rest of their lives.

This was also interwoven into the Nazi mentality before the world went to war. The public thought it was great that the state was going to be their permanent baby sitter.

It is hard to describe what was actually on Adolf's mind. He was so beloved by the masses that even he believed he was the Messiah. The "church" could not compete with Adolf even though the Catholic church said some things that were covered up for fear of reprisals. The Pope had no leverage against the Nazis since Rome was already surrounded with German troops.

Younger readers may not believe this -

BUT

History is Repeating itself

It's hard to fathom that the country is divided as it is. Looking at the 2016 Presidential election results would indicate that the liberals won the popular vote. However, estimates up to 22 million illegal votes were cast to the liberal side of the ballot. The Conservatives won the Electoral vote which is the one that put Donald Trump the winner.

Now, it would seem, that if the election wasn't rigged that Mr. Trump would have won both types of votes, making him the "popular" President.

The liberals just can't handle that. They are calling him, as well as his voters, nazis, racist, pompous, stupid, islamophobic, jerk, buffoon, deplorables and many more. They just can't come to grips that the rigged election in favor of Hillary would be won by her opponent.

Hitler did some of the same things. He put pressure of various groups to vote Nazi and there may have been some tampering of the ballots, but either way, Hitler was able to take over the government. However, there were no opponents who willingly challenged Adolf. They had been warned.

Now the liberals are "protesting" in the worst way. They are showing how childish their actions really are. Dr. Martin Luther King protested, but these liberals are RIOTING. Most are paid to act like imbeciles and they seem to be earning their money.

Chief Nazi in the US -

.. I give you George Soros. A SS in the National
Socialist German workers party. Nazi party. He served
under Adolf Hitler and Heinrich Himmler. He said it
was the best time of his life. The destruction and
agony around him was euphoric to him. This man was
making policy with Hillary Clinton. And some of you
think Trump is dangerous. Wow!

New World Order - End Times

"Remember, where you have a concentration of power in a few hands, all too frequently, men with the mentality of gangsters gain control. History has proven that...power tends to corrupt; absolute power corrupts absolutely." - British historian, Sir John Dalberg-Acton, 1887

Ron Berger

"What is at stake is more than one small

country, it is a big idea – a New World Order, where diverse nations are drawn together in a common cause, to achieve the universal aspirations of mankind; peace and security, freedom, and the rule of law… A world in which there is the very real prospect of a new world order." –President George H. W. Bush, January 29, 1991

The September 17, 1990, issue of Time magazine said that "the Bush administration would like to make the United Nations a cornerstone of its plans to construct a New World Order." Jeanne Kirkpatrick, former U.S. Ambassador to the UN, said that one of the purposes for the Desert Storm operation, was to show to the world how a "reinvigorated United Nations could serve as a global policeman in the New World Order."

The prophesied one-world government is being formed on earth at this very time. The Bible prophesies that the

Antichrist will ultimately reign over this world government for three-and-one-half years just prior to the Second Coming of Jesus to establish His own world government.

The New World Order came about as early as 1917, just after WW1. President Roosevelt talked about it in the late 30's. It came to light once President George H. W. Bush talked about it as written above. The outline for this order seem perfect, but for the fact that those that profess it being perfect are the very ones that seem to have the criminal mind when it comes to helping someone else. Rockefeller and Rothschild are the main brains behind this.

"What is the New World Order?"

The New World Order is a conspiracy theory which posts a new period of history bringing about a major change in the world with the balance of world power. This New World Order is theorized by some to involve a group or groups of elitist people bent on ruling the world through a single worldwide system of government. The appeal of this New World Order lies in its proposal to free the world of wars and political strife, and its promises to eradicate poverty, disease, and hunger. Its purpose is to meet the needs and hopes of all mankind through worldwide peace.

Also labeled the new "era of globalization," this New World Order will supposedly do away with the need for diverse world governments. This will be accomplished by the installation of a one-world political system or body. One means to achieve this is by eliminating all lines and borders demarcating the nations of the world. To effect all this change, it is believed that the New World Order will emphasize tolerance through the promotion and acceptance of other cultures and their values and ideologies. Its ultimate goal is a sense of unity and oneness with all people speaking the same language. Other objectives include the use of a single, world-wide currency, as well as oneness in politics, religion, and moral values. As a result, conspiracy theorists believe, the world will be under one rule, that of one government that promises worldwide peace, the absence of war, and the elimination of all political unrest.

Though it may be agreed that man needs hope in order to endure this life and have peace of mind, the problem lies in where man searches for such hope. The Scriptures are clear concerning all these things. As Christians, we are commanded to obey and respect those in authority, including our government. However, we can easily see that there are some severe consequences of such a New World Order, both from an economic and a religious standpoint (Romans 13:1-7; Acts 5:29).

The problem with the acceptance and approval of any New World Order is that no government has ever offered, nor will it ever offer, real hope and peace for mankind. When man turns to government to provide worldwide peace and hope, he becomes disillusioned and enslaved by its false promises. History has proven time and again that no quasi-world empire has ever survived, simply because of its innate flaws of greed, corruption, and quest for power.

Those who desire the ushering in of a New World Order, whether secular or religious, are in for a rude awakening. The truth is that false religious teachings cannot bring utopia into being, regardless of man's creativity and ingenuity. <u>Only heaven brings lasting peace and happiness.</u> The Bible makes it very clear that all things associated with this life on earth with its sufferings, its decay, its discontent, and death will continue with this physical life (2 Corinthians 4:16; Hebrews 9:27). It is *also clear that all these things are completely unknown in the heavenly city (Revelation 21:3-7 and Revelation 22). They will be done away with. Yes, hope is needed. But it is the hope of heaven we need, not the false hope of a New World Order. The one hope for all believers lies only in heaven (John 14:1-4). It is not here on this earth.*

The Clintons

Some say 33, others say 44 and still others say many more, but anyway you slice it they are TERRIBLE numbers. Nothing compared to Hitler of course, but terrible just the same.

The Clintons are the ONLY political family that have so many deaths related to people for just knowing them or having been in their company for a time. Two stand out as SUPER suspicious. Ron Brown, Bill's Secretary of

Commerce, who was reported to have died in a plane crash and Vince Foster who was on the Clinton team and rumored to have been Hillary's lover and reported to have committed suicide.

Ron Brown   Vince Foster

Strange thing - Ron was found to have a bullet hole in the back of his head at the crash scene and Vince, whose body was recently exhumed, was found to have two bullet holes in the back of his head. It's hard to call them accidents and suicides when bullets are found in the back of the head.

It needs to be noted that both had indicated that they would be "telling all" soon and the Clintons couldn't afford that.

I'm not going to talk about the "other" accidents, murders or suicides that are related to the Clintons, but the list is long and it starts with two young boys in Arkansas, when Bill was Attorney General, who saw to much and ends up recently as close workers on Hillary's 2016 campaign. So many people having heart attacks or committing suicide and no one is looking into these deaths over this length of time.

They are as good as Adolf was in making sure their fingerprints were never found at the scene. The Arkansas Mofia stayed with the Clintons and carried out their wishes.

"Here, ruining people is considered sport" Vince Foster

> *Presidents Andrew Johnson and Bill Clinton were impeached by the U.S. House of Representatives, but acquitted by the Senate. Richard Nixon resigned before he could be impeached.*

Yes - the above statement is true. Isn't that a terrible anchor to be tied around your neck? It hasn't seemed to slow down the most notorious womanizer to ever occupy the Presidency.

Bill started way back in Arkansas when he was the Attorney General. Once he became Governor the frequency of his philandering sped up. Nothing stopped him when he became President and even after he has been associated with pedophilia with many trips to "sex island".

Hillary has stood up for Bill, but she also has been rumored to have visited "sex island" several times. She has also been accused of having sexual relationships with a number of men as well as women.

The Clintons seemed to have placed themselves so far above everyone else that the law just wouldn't go after them. The flawed 2016 Presidential run really opened up the sins that the Clintons seem to be guilty of. Even the attempts from Bill to redirect any inquiry into Hillary's problems that were brought to light didn't seem to rattle the liberals. Even the FBI seems to have succumbed to Bill's pressures.

Bill & Hillary have carried on with their life like there will never be a day of judgement. Bill has had numerous affairs, before, during and after being President and Hillary has also had some along with her ever present lying. Both have much to answer for and that's not even considering all the questionable deaths related to them.

Being a friend to the Clintons is not a long term relationship if you seem to cross them in any way.

Hitler was the same way about those that might cross him. He only had one bad experience when his niece, with whom he had an affair, committed suicide(?). He swore off women saying, "he was married to Germany".

Adolf had no remorse when he had others killed. He just figured that it was a cost to make Germany the only country in the world, with him as it's leader.

You don't hear much about Bill wanting to make a "New World Order". but you can bet that with him and George H.W. Bush being such great friends, this was the tying knot in their relationship. Even though Bill beat H.W. for the Presidency.

Between (about) 1990 and 2016 the popularity of a one world government reached it's high point. Combining the efforts of the Rockefeller's, Rothschild's, Bush's, Clinton's and Obama's the one world government wasn't far from their lips. Of course, they all wanted to be the big cheese and run the world.

Hillary's flawed run for the Presidency in 2008 started the ball rolling for her to commit so many sins that they still haven't all been accounted for.

Being pressured by BO to cast her vote for him with the promise that after eight years she would replace him was to big a bargain to bypass.

BO got the nod and Hillary became Secretary of State where she could do all sorts of damage to the country's reputation and line her pockets at the same time. She received more help from foreign countries than was ever previously known. She and Bill also set up the *"Clinton Foundation"* and granted favors to those countries that contributed. Millions poured in and only a very small percentage went to help the needy - to make it a tax deductible charity.   The majority ended up in their pockets.

The Man with the
Golden Tongue

Yes - Adolf had a golden tongue. He was able to mesmerize people and won them over with his diatribe. In all honesty, the people of Germany were looking for a *"savior"*, especially after the 1929 stock market crash which set the whole world back. Adolf was the man to save the common folk.

Barack Hussein Obama - enters the picture in 2008 from a background so obscure that no one ever heard of him. He had a little time in the Senate, but accomplished nothing except preparing to run for the Presidency.

BO had trouble, in the beginning, speaking and needed a teleprompter on all occasions. Finally he got the hang of it and figured out how to read quite well. He had a voice that you didn't mind listening to, until you heard what he had to say. His youthful appearance, first black to make it (although he's half white) and a good command of the English language (although it was all written out for him on the teleprompter). He was *different* than all that came before him. Some even said he had to many "girlish" gestures. Maybe thats why the women went for him at the voting booth.

BO won over the hearts of the DNC and had backers like Senator Ted Kennedy. The big question still was - *"who the h*ll is Barack Hussein Obama?"*

Not until years later did we find out that he was a "nobody" who happened to be financed by George Soros. He was even able to buy off Hillary in 2008 so he could win the nomination.

This is pretty much how Adolf started out in politics. The people had heard of him, but paid him no mind until the economic bottom fell out. Then he still had trouble since he was associated with "rough necks" and the voters didn't like that. Then he figured out how to be a politician and tell the people what they wanted to hear. He posed himself as "one of them" and the people fell for it, hook line an sinker.

The Nazi Ideology

The Nazi party didn't start off big, but rather in the back room of a beer joint. Workers were fed up with the government and wanted some changes. They also had a deep hatred toward the Jews and Communists.

This all followed Adolf's thinking as well and he started speaking and railing against their common hates. This small group was custom matched to Hitler and he reveled in it. He soon became their leader.

Hate has a tendency to grow quickly among common haters. They soon changed their name from the German Workers' Party to the National Socialist German Workers' Party or more commonly called the Nazi party.

From the early 1920's until the early 30's the party grew and faltered depending on the national needs. They were not needed when the going was good, but called upon when the going was rough.

Hitler struggled in the beginning and made some big mistakes and ended up in jail. With his gift of gab and his appealing diatribe he was able to convince the judge to a much leaner sentence than his crime demanded. It was actually a blessing for him because it gave him time to plan and then write his *"Mein Kampf" (my struggle)*.

ON APRIL I, 1924, because of the sentence handed down by the People's Court of Munich, I had to begin that day, serving my term in the fortress at Landsberg on the Lech.

Thus, after years of uninterrupted work, I was afforded for the first time an opportunity to embark on a task insisted upon by many and felt to be serviceable to the movement by myself. Therefore, I resolved not only to set forth, in two volumes, the object of our movement, but also to draw a picture of its development. From this more can be learned than from any purely doctrinary treatise.

That also gave me the opportunity to describe my own development, as far as this is necessary for the understanding of the first as well as the second volume, and which may serve to destroy the evil legends created about my person by the Jewish press.

With this work I do not address myself to strangers, but to those adherents of the movement who belong to it with their hearts and whose reason now seeks a more intimate enlightenment. I know that one is able to win people far more by the spoken than by the written word, and that every great movement on this globe owes its rise to the great speakers and not to the great writers.

Nevertheless, the basic elements of a doctrine must be set down in permanent form in order that it may be represented in the same way and in unity. In this connection these two volumes should serve as building stones which I add to our common work.

THE AUTHOR

LANDSBERG ON THE LECH
PRISON OF THB FORTRESS

This preface was Adolf's to start his book. His entire book deals with what he believed Germany should do to be great and to eliminate those that, he felt, dragged it down. Not many people read the book in the beginning and only after he became *"Der Führer"* did the sales pick up. In fact, it was required reading. If the Allies had read it then, WW11 may not have happened.

Hitler found out that being a "tough guy" was a turn-off to the voting public and his only other course of action was to become a politician. That way he could use his gift of oratory to sway the public to his way of thinking. There were plenty of ups and downs and the real turn of events happened when the stock market crashed in 1929 effecting the entire world.

Now the people started to take Adolf seriously. His popularity grew quickly. Seemingly he had the words that the voting public wanted to hear. The Nazi party quickly grew to become one of the largest parties in Germany.

Now in 1932 the government was realizing that he was a force to reckon with. Adolf Hitler is named chancellor of Germany on Jan 30, 1933 and with the death of German President Paul von Hindenburg, Chancellor Adolf Hitler becomes absolute dictator of Germany under the title of Führer.

This is the point in time that the innocents of Adolf is left behind. He took away the freedoms the people had under the ruse that it was for their own good as well as the country's. Still he told the people to give him four years and he will have Germany back in the black again. Actually the only thing black was the uniforms of his special forces - the SS (The Schutzstaffel). They started out as his personal body guards and then expanded into military units.

These were the highly trained "killers" that Adolf made plans for in the annihilation of his political opponents, Jews, Communists, homosexuals, Gypsies and any other groups that were a threat to him. Catholics became part of that list as well, but not so much at first.

The people had no idea of Adolf's inner thoughts and only listened to his spoken words. Hitler showed them that his reforms were working and the country began to heal itself. Of course he didn't tell them that he was secretly building up the armed forces and making plans to expand the "home front" (lebensraum).

By this time the killing was starting to take place, but was so secret that very few knew about it. Those that suspected or had knowledge of these killings were easily talked into believing that it was for the better since they were "vermin" anyway.

Once Adolf invaded Poland, the killing camps were placed there and the German people felt better to know that it wasn't happening in their country. This is also when the Nazis started their killing of Catholic priests. Usually the special SS troops followed the infantry and did the dirty work. However, when the progress moved faster than the SS could keep up, the regular army troops filled in and did the killing.

When the tide of war started to go against the Nazis and they started to retreat, they finished the killing and burning that they didn't have time for when they were going forward.

The estimates of the slaughter range anywhere up to 50 million men, women and children. Those that weren't systematically killed in the concentration camps were actively silenced by their neighbors or whoever had the hankering, because they thought they were doing what the Führer wanted.

The Gestapo was very instrumental in pitting the children against their parents and neighbor against neighbor. Many were arrested and never seen again. Such brutality became second nature to the majority of citizens and they had no idea to the extent the horror was. Large dugouts were made in the earth and filled with bodies - some still alive. Everywhere the Nazis went there were fields that hundreds and thousands of bodies were buried.

Many of those who orchestrated these deaths testified later that they didn't know what they were doing and were just following orders. This period in history is so blood stained that it is truly hard to digest it all and understand it. It is beyond normal comprehension. No person in their right mind would go along with this program - OR WOULD THEY?

After these concentration camps were uncovered at war's end, General Eisenhower insisted that all the surrounding neighbors of the camp walk through and look at what their "leaders" did. Many looked shocked and still many, I'm sure, satisfied their thoughts after the smell of burning bodies and the endless trains of people being brought in, but not out, aroused their suspicions. Dare they call themselves FOOLS for falling for the lies they were told. I would say that would be the kindest word they could use.

Todays Nazis

The American Nazi Party (ANP) was first an American political party founded by George Lincoln Rockwell. Its headquarters were in Arlington, Virginia. Rockwell founded the organization as the World Union of Free Enterprise National Socialists (WUFENS), but renamed it the American Nazi Party in 1960.[2] The party was based largely upon the ideals and policies of Adolf Hitler's Nazi Party in Germany during the Nazi era, and embraced its uniforms and iconography.[3][A]

The Rockwell organization broke up shortly after he was assassinated in 1967. Since the late 1960s, there have been a number of small groups that have used the name, "American Nazi Party".

The American Nazi Party is in no way comparable to the one founded by Adolf.

However, their beliefs are the same and their hatred of the Jew and Blacks is comparable to the intensity found in the 30's and 40's in Germany. They believe that only the "whites" should live in America.

Their ideology is still fascist in nature as it was in Hitler's day. *German Fascism. Once in power, Adolf Hitler turned Germany into a fascist state. Fascist was originally used to describe the government of Benito Mussolini in Italy. Mussolini's fascist one-party state emphasized patriotism, national unity, hatred of communism, admiration of military values and unquestioning obedience.*

Most of today's Nazis I really considered middlemen. These are the kind of people that when given orders we'll go out and riot and burn and harass others that don't fall in line with their own thinking.

GEORGE SOROS'S SIX

@USAFORTRUMP

REPUBLICANS FUNDED BY GEORGE SOROS TO POTENTIALLY TAKE OUT TRUMP

When you hear people calling others Nazis, all you have to do is see that they're more Nazi than those they are accusing. They do that to throw you off the track. They want you to look at the accused rather than themselves.

Everyone pictured above has large connections to the Nazi mentality with one exception and that's George Soros who is the head Nazi in America.

First you have those that pretend to be all American, but in actuality fall short of that title. The Republicans shown, are considered RINO's or Republicans in name only. These are the worst since they are deceiving the general public and in fact, doing irreparable damage to our entire country. They are the ones that are hell-bent on taking down the administration and actually siding with the enemies of the state.

Other Main RINO's

1. Sen. Lincoln Chafee (R.I.)
Once approached by Democratic
Leader Harry Reid to switch parties,
Chafee has long supported liberal

policies. He backs legal abortion, gay rights, federal-funded health care, strict environmental protections and a higher minimum wage. Opposes ANWR drilling. Also was the only Republican in Congress not to endorse the President's reelection and one of three who tried to gut Bush's tax cuts.

2. Sen. Olympia Snowe (Maine)
A self-described "centrist," Snowe scored a 100% pro-choice voting record as scored by NARAL and consistently votes with Democrats on social issues.

3. Sen. Arlen Specter (Pa.)
"Snarlin' Arlen" warned Bush not to nominate judges who might overturn Roe v. Wade, joined Chaffee reducing tax cuts and supported Democrats on the Comprehensive Test Ban Treaty,

HMO and overtime regulation. Also opposed school choice in Washington, D.C.

4. Sen. Susan Collins (Maine)
Voted with liberals on the 1999 tax cut, campaign finance reform and the partial-birth abortion ban. Also advocated "pay-as-you-go" tax cuts with spending increases in 2004, leading to a budget never agreed upon between the House and Senate.

5. Rep. Christopher Shays (Conn.)
He led the House fight for McCain-Feingold campaign finance "reform." He's also prone to back environmental causes, gun control and abortion rights. He had no GOP challenger in 2004, but narrowly escaped defeat, 52% to 48%,

by a Democratic opponent in the general election.

6. Gov. George Pataki (N.Y.)
Helped unions raise pay and unionize Indian casinos. Has said, "I believe in a limited government, low taxes, a tough approach to crime. … But I also believe in an activist government. I'm not one of those laissez-faire types."

7. Rep. Sherwood Boehlert (N.Y.)
Over the course of his 23-year career, he's gained considerable power (chairman of the Science Committee), despite amassing one of the most liberal voting records of any House Republican. Fought back conservative challengers in 2000 and 2002 and could face a GOP challenge in '06.

8. Gov. Mitt Romney (Mass.)
Has said, "I believe that abortion should be safe and legal in this country." Supports civil unions and stringent gun laws. After visiting Houston, he criticized the city's aesthetics, saying, "This is what happens when you don't have zoning."

9. Rep. Michael Castle (Del.)
As president of the moderate Republican Main Street Partnership and key player in the so-called Tuesday Group lunches, he is a ring-leader of RINOs. He's teamed with Democrats to make federal funding of embryonic stem cell research one of his top priorities.

10. Rep. Jim Leach (Iowa)
One of only six House Republicans to vote against the Iraq War resolution in

2002, he was also the only Republican to vote against President Bush's 2003 tax cuts. His support for environmental causes and abortion rights has won him liberal fans. disdain for the Recognition of Human Rights - Because of fear of enemies and the need for security, the people in fascist regimes are persuaded that human rights can be ignored in certain cases because of "need." The people tend to look the other way or even approve of torture, summary executions, assassinations, long incarcerations of prisoners, etc.

Nazi Traits

Hate: Hitler used hate as a tool to rile up the citizens to hate those that he considered inferior. Much hate is used today toward conservatives who won the election even after all the cheating at the poles.

Those that profess hatred toward anyone is as guilty of evil as they profess their accused of. Those that hate are not expressing their own feelings mainly, but rather that of those that are paying them. Those that hate are worse than a murderer.

Blame: Hitler blamed the Jews for losing the First World War. He was shocked when he heard Germany had surrendered as he lay in his hospital bed. He truly believed that the government capitulated to the demands of the Jews and stopped the war. That was the biggest dagger in his heart. From then on the Jews were the main reason for all his terrible acts.

We heard this blame element often during the eight years of Barack Hussein Obama. Everything that caught the attention of the public that wasn't right automatically was blamed on the previous President. Bush was to blame for so many things that you lost count.

We are now finding out who we should blame for all the wrongs that have been perpetrated on our country. The Democratic Party has "gone over" to the other side and left their followers in the dust. They are losing those that really felt that they were following a party that cared about the average American. They are now learning that being progressive isn't the positive way of doing things.

Lying: Hitler lied telling his people what he had up his sleeve. Every time he made a speech he would tell them his actions were for their own good. It took them several years to realized that being boomed daily was not for their own good.

This is a trait that surfaced early and continually during the run up to the election. Many accused then candidate Trump of lying about something, but we later found out that they lied about lying. Now they are accusing President Trump again as another excuse for losing the battle. One thing they haven't been able to do is stand in front of a mirror and say - WE LOST!

Terror: Hitler used terror to keep everyone on their toes. He would burn Temples and Churches, stores and homes and kill people just for the fun of it. People feared the Gestapo and SS and when they were around something bad would happen.

The same thing is happening now with all the "Black Lives Matter" type groups that burn, loot and riot in the streets of many US cities. They are spreading terror throughout the country and are being paid by the "head Nazi". Most are afraid of "offending" groups like this that they would rather suffer at their brutal hands than call a spade a spade. We Americans fall in the category of fear of offending and willing to suffer for it. It's time we all stood up to these groups and hit back. We already have a President on our side and now we need to treat these evil elements to cut and run or get on board.

Slander: Adolf used this to maximize his description of the "inferiors". It was so ingrained in the everyday talk of the population that the Jews were nothing but vermin. Therefore the Führer must be right in his treatment of the Jews, Communists and any others that he didn't like.

In all the years that I've watched a new President take office (13), I have never heard so much slanderous gossip as I have with President Trump. It has to be because he is rich, non politician who no one thought could win, but did. Donald reached the hearts of the mainstream American and earned their vote. He proved that the existing government was corrupt and almost beyond saving. So far he is the only candidate ever, that is trying to honor all his campaign promises.

Control of the Media: Hitler used the media to his best advantage. Nothing was allowed to reach the public's ears that wasn't first cleared with his Propaganda Minister, Paul Joseph Goebbels. Goebbels was in charge of all communication for the Third Reich, including any words about the Führer himself. Hitler relied on Goebbels to set the stage in the most enduring way so that Adolf would have a much easier time of it.

The present day news media is now filled with **"fake news"** and it's impossible to rely on anything you hear or see on the news. It's terrible to see that President Trump relies of "twitter" to get his word out when the press says little or nothing about it.

Corruption: Corruption is something that every government and large organization are cursed with. *Adolf Hitler came to power by means of wits, not only was he very intelligent but he had a plan, and executed it. He preyed on the weak and vulnerable, setting up alliances with people in high places to do the 'dirty work'. Thus securing his long time invasion plans. With most of Germany in a financial crisis and in fear of losing jobs Hitler decided to pounce. He told them that by joining forces with him, Germany would gain power, a power that had never been witnessed before. This movement began to gain momentum and before anyone knew it, the Nazi's had gained power in parliament. Hitler was to be crowned chancellor, shortly before the president died in 1934. He reigned supreme in the race for presidency and took charge of the 'monster movement'. Germany had no idea of what was yet to come, thinking that this would be a change for* *the better. It was the calm before the storm.*

This is a different kind of corruption than we are accustom to. Most corruption is the cheating and stealing that happens by those we trust. Our Congress is littered with many corrupted representatives that we may never hear about. These are the two faced people that tell you you how honest they are until you find out how much they have stollen.

Finally the -

Coup
de gras

*Germany lost the war
but-
the Nazis didn't*

Ron Berger

ISIS

The recent report by Transparency International, "the Big Spin", according to the BBC, carries an objective insight into the questions of ISIS, Terrorism, and Extremism; no politicization or biases.

The Big Spin found that ISIS cannot be defeated without addressing the enabling factors of corruption, which allow for terrorist groups to grow and expand. It accuses western states, too, including the US and UK, of ignoring corruption as an enabler it is of terrorism.

Apparently; the organization exploits corruption to spread its seeds, introducing itself as the antidote to corruption while seeking to cover up his own acts of ilk, which is nothing new to us.

Ron Berger

Katherine Dixon, Director of the Transparency International organization's Defense and Security, reaffirmed the report's findings.
Corruption is a rallying cry, an enabler and a key modus operandi for ISIS. The failure to grasp this undermines efforts to tackle the rise of violent extremism. The international community expends great efforts tackling the 'ideology' of groups such as ISIS, focusing on the religious rhetoric they produce, yet completely ignoring the material circumstances in which they thrive. Corruption is a real security threat, more than just a means for elites to line their pockets. In the end corrupt governments by fueling public anger and undermining institutions, are the architects of their own security crises.

his is not just about closing off the corrupt channels that enable the day-to-day operations of groups like ISIS, but rethinking relationships with the

Mubaraks, Gadhafis and Malikis of the future.

To the BBC, Dixon underscored that "corruption is a real security threat, more than just a means for elites to line their pockets. In the end corrupt governments by fueling public anger and undermining institutions, are the architects of their own security crises."

Rightly, the report ties the rise of radicalism in the Arab World to corruption, and underlines the necessity to address it as the grave and concrete danger it is; both domestically and regionally.

Corruption undermines the political institution from the inside and poisons the public's relationship with it, which platforms nepotism and social frustration, escalates unrest, and reinforces a mass sense of social injustice and inequality, which is only the precursor to lawlessness.

Notably, that would uproot any political system, no matter how stable!
This is —as coined in the report— ISIS's Big Spin; their ilk's ability to recruit and exploit the public's outcry at their deteriorated situations by investing it in a promotional spin to present themselves as remedy or alternative.

Agreeably, corruption is tied to autocracy, dictatorship, and the lack of accountability and transparency, which usually go hand in hand with violations in human rights and public liberties, including freedom of the press and the rights of expression.

Accordingly, the report sees that corruption is a subsequent product of dictatorship, and hence calls to revaluate relationships with autocratic states.

Whereas other factors of culture and ideology stand just as well, the report only validates what we have been saying for years: that ISIS is the product of autocracy and the absence of democracy.

Additionally, perhaps one the most crucial points featured in the report is the fact that the terrorist group is indeed presenting itself as an alternative, wrapped in a religions cloak, pretexted by the proposition of their "utopian" state.

As fragile and unrealistic as that may seem to us; it is viable for vast segments of society, including youth, who are incapable of embracing and reconciling with their worsening reality. Hence, comes the promise of the ideal state, by ISIS and similar terrorist organizations.

There lies the core and primary danger of the organization and its ideology. Even if it were militarily vanquished, and its delusionary Caliphate destroyed, it is not so difficult to reconstruct it virtually or maybe even physically; somewhere else.

More dangerously, if we do not address the faults of our systems now, then the next coming of ISIS will be fiercer and far more destructive!

ISIS is the modern day Nazi. During the Second World War, Hitler and the Grand Mufti Haj Amin al-Husseini became friends since they both hated the Jews and sought ways to eliminate them.

According to some reports, the CIA invented ISIS. Hard to believe, but wouldn't put it past them.

ISIS is relatively new to the world of terror, but the Nazis are the founder of the modern day terror groups.

During the last two years of World WarII, the Nazis, realizing that the war wasn't going in their favor, put together a group known as "werwolf". These were younger males, some from the military, to continue the policies of the Nazis when the war was lost. Under the evil eye of Heinrich Himmler, *Rumors of a secret Nazi guerrilla organization began to surface soon after the Allied invasion of Normandy. TIME magazine ran an article containing speculation that the Germans would try to prolong the war indefinitely by going underground after their defeat.[9] The January 27, 1945 issue of Collier's Weekly featured a detailed article by Major Edwin Lessner, stating that elite SS and Hitler Youth were being trained to attack Allied forces and opening with a 1944 quote from Joseph Goebbels: "The enemy (invading German territory) will be taken in the rear by the fanatical population, which will ceaselessly worry him, tie down strong forces and allow him no rest or exploitation of any possible success."*

On March 23, 1945, Goebbels gave a speech known as the "Werwolf speech", in which he urged every German to fight to the death. The partial dismantling of the organized Werwolf, combined with the effects of the Werwolf speech, caused considerable confusion about which subsequent attacks were actually carried out by Werwolf members, as opposed to solo acts by fanatical Nazis or small groups of SS.

Otto Skorzeny (12 June 1908 – 5 July 1975) was an Austrian SS-Obersturmbannführer (lieutenant colonel) in the German Waffen-SS during World War II. During the war, he was involved in a string of operations, including the rescue mission that freed the deposed Italian dictator Benito Mussolini from captivity. Skorzeny led Operation Greif, in which German soldiers infiltrated enemy lines using their opponents' languages, uniforms, and customs. For this he was charged at the Dachau Military Tribunal with breaching the 1907 Hague Convention, but was acquitted. At the end of the war, Skorzeny was involved with the Werwolf guerrilla movement.

Skorzeny escaped from an internment camp in 1948, hiding out on a Bavarian farm for 18 months, then spent time in Paris and Salzburg before eventually settling in Spain. In 1953 he became a military advisor to Egyptian President Mohammed Naguib and recruited a staff of former SS and Wehrmacht officers to train the Egyptian Army, staying on to advise President Gamal Abdel Nasser. In 1962, Skorzeny was recruited by the Mossad and conducted operations for the agency. He spent time in Argentina, where he acted as an advisor to President Juan Perón and as a bodyguard for Eva Perón. Skorzeny died of lung cancer on 5 July 1975 in Madrid. He was 67.

Otto was named by Hitler as the leader of the werwolfs. One of his first activities was to infiltrate behind the Allied lines at the Battle of the Bulge and cause chaos to disrupt the defense poised by the Americans.

Otto had taught all the terror dirty tricks known to man and they set about doing their dirty work. The operation at the Battle of the Bulge was first exposed to us in the movie. How dare the Nazis sabotage our forces.

Otto managed to escape sentencing by breaking out of jail, after the war, and hiding out and moving to various countries. He ended up in Egypt teaching large classes of would be terrorists such as: Mohammed **Yasser** Abdel Rahman Abdel Raouf **Arafat** al-Qudwa future PLO leader, **Muammar** Mohammed Abu Minyar **Gaddaf**i the future dictator from Libya, **Hosni Mubarak** the future President of Egypt and **Saddam Hussein** soon to be dictator in Iraq. Quite an alumni.

Many of these "leaders" are responsible for forming some of the most ruthless terror organizations the world has ever known. They are:

Al-Qaeda - (2)
ISIS - (1)
Taliban - (3)
Hezbollah - (5)
Hamas
Boko Haram - (4)
Al-shabaab - (6)

(size) I'm sure you have heard of a few of these organizations. If not - YOU'RE THE PROBLEM.

Many people, especially the younger people, have trouble visualizing how bad terrorism can be. War is a form of terrorism, but it's not labeled as such.

WWI was a good example of the terror in terrorism. Two opposing armies facing each other, about several hundred yards apart, each side deep in their own trenches that may have a foot of water and rotting bodies. The whistle blows and they are up out of the trenches running to certain death. Each side takes turns doing this. Hundreds are slaughtered and if a bullet doesn't get you some disease will.

WWII was a little more sophisticated whereas the troops were loaded into landing craft and when they were offloaded on the beach as the machine-guns were mowing them down. Or - just just having breakfast in the mess hall and have the Japanese bomb your ship.

I know that there are not many civilian caparisons to war unless you remember 9/11/01. Thousands had just reported to work in the Trade Center Twin Towers in New York and lo and behold a commercial jet rams the building. It didn't hit the top floor, but the 80th floor of a 110 story building. This cut off hundreds of people from escaping. Many died of burns and some even jumped out the windows. Image jumping that high without a parachute just knowing that you will die.

The second plane crashed in the south tower around the 60th floor, again cutting off an escape route for hundreds of people. More than 3,000 people died because 19 terrorists wanted it. Just place yourself in one of these buildings - even below the impact areas and then having the entire building fall all around you. **This is terror**!

It doesn't matter what organization was responsible for this disaster. They all pretty much operate on the same principal - kill as many infidels as you can. Those that believe that Islam is a peaceful religion are wrong on two counts. One, they are not peaceful and two - the are not religious. Any group that uses the Koran and Mohammad's words as their justification to kill is a murderer. Killing infidels (those that don't believe in the Koran) is the sickest reason to take someone's life.

Those that get "tricked" into joining ISIS have very little gray matter to deal with anyway. The girls that fall in "love" with these idiots think it's smart and that they will be riding in the catbird's seat. They soon find out that they are treated like so much trash.

Even some Hollywood celebrities believe the women in the Muslim world have more rights than American women are more than a brick short of a load. It's sickening to hear of people, who have experienced freedom, who want to join a terrorist group.

Nazi Germany was very much the same way. The power of the spoken word initiated a mass exodus from sane people to blinded people.

People You may Know & Love?

No Wonder Liberals Are So Confused !

Black — Indian — Woman

Reverend — Scientist — Journalist

Honest — Presidential — Husband

Rachel Dolezal, the infamous white woman who for years passed herself off as African American and rose to become head of an NAACP branch, is now jobless, on food stamps and expects to soon be homeless.

A defiant Dolezal, 39, recounted her current plight to The Guardian. Dolezal said she's only been offered jobs in reality television and porno flicks. A friend helped her come up with the money for February's rent and she doesn't know how she's going to pay for March and she still says she's not white.

Despite a nearly three week flap over her claim of "being Native American," the progressive consumer advocate has been unable to point to evidence of Native heritage except for a unsubstantiated thirdhand report that she might be 1/32 Cherokee. Even if it could be proven, it wouldn't qualify her to be a member of a tribe: Contrary to assertions in outlets from The New York Times to Mother Jones that having 1/32 Cherokee ancestry is "sufficient for tribal citizenship," "Indian enough" for "the Cherokee Nation," and "not a deal-breaker," Warren would not be eligible to

become a member of any of the three federally recognized Cherokee tribes based on the evidence so far surfaced by independent genealogists about her ancestry.

Jenner has six children from marriages to wives Chrystie Crownover, Linda Thompson, and Kris Jenner. Since 2007, Jenner has appeared on the reality television series Keeping Up with the Kardashians with Kris, their daughters Kendall and Kylie Jenner, and step-children Kourtney, Kim, Khloé, and Rob Kardashian. Previously identifying publicly as male, Jenner revealed her identity as a <u>trans woman</u>

in April 2015, publicly announcing her name change from Bruce to Caitlyn in a July 2015 Vanity Fair cover story. Her name and gender change became official on September 25, 2015.[8] She has been called the most famous openly transgender woman in the world.[9][10] [11]From 2015 to 2016, Jenner starred in the reality television series I Am Cait, which focused on her gender transition.

On 18 November 2014, the New York Times published an article titled "As Sharpton Rose, So Did His Unpaid Taxes" asserting

more than $4.5 million in current state and federal tax liens had been taken out against the civil rights activist and his for-profit businesses. That item echoed a previous article <u>published</u> *in August of 2014 by the New York Post titled "Sharpton Demands Accountability, But Still Owes Millions in Back Taxes." Both articles stated records reviewed by the respective publications showed Sharpton owed millions of dollars to state and federal agencies in unpaid taxes, with the Post reporting: Sharpton himself owes New York state $806,875 and has federal liens for unpaid personal income taxes against him totaling $2.6 million, records show.*

Al Gore is known for his belief in global warming.

S. Fred Singer is a distinguished astrophysicist who has taken a hard, scientific look at the evidence. In this book, Dr. Singer explores the inaccuracies in historical climate data, the limitations of attempting to model climate on computers, solar variability and its impact on climate, the effects of clouds, ocean currents, and sea levels on global climate, and factors that could mitigate any human impacts on world climate.

Singer's masterful analysis decisively shows that the pessimistic, and often alarming, global warming scenarios depicted in the media have no scientific basis. In fact, he finds that many aspects of any global warming, such as a longer growing season for food and a reduced need to use fossil fuels for heating, would actually have a positive impact on the human race. Further, Singer notes how many proposed "solutions" to the global warming "crisis" (like "carbon" taxes) would have severe consequences for economically disadvantaged groups and nations.

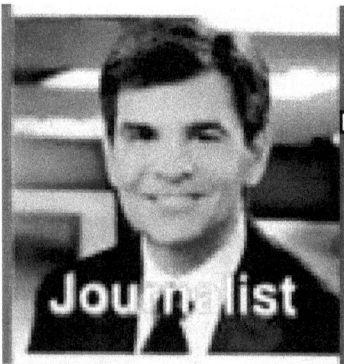

George Robert Stephanopoulos (born February 10, 1961) is an American journalist and former political advisor. Stephanopoulos is currently the

Chief Anchor and the Chief Political Correspondent for ABC News, a co-anchor of Good Morning America, and the host of ABC's Sunday morning This Week. Stephanopoulos is a regular substitute anchor for ABC World News Tonight.

Prior to his career as a journalist, Stephanopoulos was an advisor to the Democratic Party. He rose to early prominence as a Communications Director for the 1992 U.S. Presidential Campaign of Bill Clinton and subsequently became White House Communications Director. He was later Senior Advisor for Policy and Strategy before departing in December 1996. Stephanopoulos is a member of the Council on Foreign Relations.

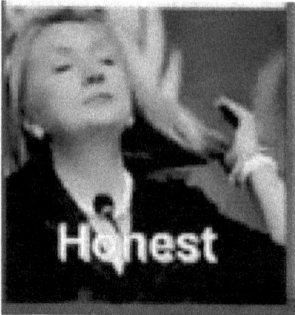

In 1996, the New Yorker published **"Hating Hillary,"** Henry Louis Gates' reported piece on the widespread animosity for the then–first lady. "Like horse-racing, Hillary-hating has become one of those national pastimes which unite the élite and the lumpen," Gates wrote. "[T]here's just something about her that pisses people off," the renowned Washington hostess Sally Quinn told Gates. "This is the reaction that she elicits from people."

*It might seem as though nothing much has changed in 20 years. Many people disliked Hillary Clinton when she first emerged onto the political scene, and many people dislike her now. She is on track to become the **least popular** Democratic nominee in modern history.*

<u>Barack Obama</u> took his first step back onto the world stage on

Tuesday, shedding his tie to give wide-ranging, if studiously nonpartisan, remarks during a food and technology conference in Milan.

First in a keynote address, during which he often consulted his notes, and then in a policy-heavy conversation with <u>his former chef, Sam Kass</u>, Mr. Obama spoke about how climate change was imperiling food production around the world and threatening to aggravate the "migration that has put such a burden on Europe."

In a conversation that seemed intended to avoid making news, he also spoke about rain patterns, income inequality, privacy issues, his post-presidential life and cows. When President Trump was mentioned, Mr. Obama politely turned the page, saying that while "the current administration has differences with my administration in terms of energy policy," he believed that "the private sector has already made a decision that the future is in clean energy."

Since leaving office, Mr. Obama has kitesurfed with the billionaire Richard Branson, started writing his memoirs and begun earning speaking fees. Critics have accused Mr. Obama, who campaigned as a different kind of politician, of hypocrisy for accepting an offer of $400,000 to speak in September at a health care conference run by the Wall Street firm Cantor Fitzgerald.

*The **impeachment of Bill Clinton** was initiated by the House of Representatives on December 19, 1998, against Bill Clinton, the 42nd President of the United States, on two charges, one of perjury and one of obstruction of justice. These charges stemmed from Clinton's extramarital affair with former White House Intern Monica Lewinsky and his testimony about the affair during a sexual harassment lawsuit filed against him by Paula Jones. Clinton was subsequently acquitted of these charges by the Senate on February 12, 1999. Two other impeachment articles – a second perjury charge and a charge of abuse of power – failed in the House.*

The trial in the United States Senate began right after the seating of the 106th Congress, in which the Republican Party began with 55 senators. A two-thirds vote (67 senators) was required to remove Clinton from office. Fifty senators voted to remove Clinton on the obstruction of justice charge and 45 voted to remove him on the perjury charge; no member of his own Democratic Party voted guilty on either charge. Clinton, like Johnson a century earlier, was acquitted on all charges.

Truly a miscarriage of justice

WE ARE LEADERS

@USAForTRUMP

OF THE PARTY OF HATE, DIVISION & DESTRUCTION

All are guilty of corruption

Watch out for these
True RINO's

Remembering what I lived through and my upbringing, I would have trouble calling any of these people, Nazi. I believe that to be the most hated word I could use, but many of them have no trouble calling others this foul name.

These people are typical of what a turn-coat would call another American in a liberal vs conservative discussion. These RINO's need to be watched because of their tendencies to use Nazi deception, half truth or fake news.

Propaganda is defined as: *"information, especially of a biased or misleading nature, used to promote a political cause or point of view". Propaganda is often associated with the psychological mechanisms of influencing and altering the attitude of a population toward a specific cause, position or political agenda in an effort to form a consensus to a standard set of belief patterns.[2] Propaganda is information that is not objective and is used primarily to influence an audience and further an agenda, often by presenting facts selectively (perhaps lying by omission) to encourage a particular synthesis or perception, or using loaded messages or "loaded language" to produce an emotional rather than a rational response to the information that is presented. Propaganda is often associated with material prepared by governments, but activist groups and companies can also produce propaganda.*

These people have been known to do that many times lately. And, even though I voted for John McCain in 2008, I now believe the best thing he brought to his campaign was Sarah Palin.

1. Sen. John McCain, (R-AZ)

I do not want to minimize the pain and suffering that John went through in his 5-1/2 years as a POW in the Viet Nam War. Spending a day in North Viet Nam would be all I could muster.

There have been stories that he received favored treatment because his Father was an Admiral in the US Navy, He was offered early release from the Hanoi Hilton, but he refused it since others had been there longer and should also be released. The torture that he went through, as well as most of the other POW's, should not be forced on any person or animal. There was nothing humane in his treatment.

I voted for John McCain when he ran for President in 2008. I felt he was much more qualified than BO. Actually I was really voting for Sarah Palin. At that time John didn't have the backing of George Soros and his money.

Today is a different story. John has been a loyal supporter of BO for a number of years - probably ever since he received the first Soros' check. John has balked at nearly everything President Trump is trying to do. He is a "turncoat" Republican and would do better if he changed parties.

John's beliefs go back a ways to when he was in the company of G. Gordon Liddy. Here is a synopsis of what he believes taken from 2008:   *John McCain claimed that G. Gordon Liddy paid his debt to society and so his association with Liddy is perfectly alright. Yet, Liddy has never recanted the claims made in his book or the claims made in the article in The Independent. That John McCain would claim that G. Gordon Liddy's principles and philosophies "make this nation great", is truly frightening. Does McCain truly believe in these things and if so, don't we need to know about it?*

These brave men did not risk their lives so that the likes of G. Gordon Liddy and John McCain could embrace the philosophies and principles of Nazism.

Make no mistake: John McCain knows exactly what G. Gordon Liddy's principles and philosophies are. So do Karl Rove, Dick Cheney and the rest of the Republican hierarchy. John McCain has had ample opportunity to distance himself from G. Gordon Liddy and his principles and philosophies and yet he continues to maintain that his association with Liddy is just fine.

I would never accuse anyone of being a Nazi, but there are those that maintain a strong feeling and a forceful attitude toward the Nazi cause.

2. House Speaker Paul Ryan (R-WI)

Ron Berger   107

Paul Ryan is married to Janna Little a liberal, left wing progressive, anti-Constitutional, big government George Soros supporter who voted for Barack Hussein Obama twice.

Whether true or not, she is a Democrat and comes from a liberal family and I'm sure this is enough to help influence Paul's thinking.

Paul has been a RINO since his lost election as a VP candidate with Mitt Romney in 2012. He has switched positions several times on backing the present President.

Paul's 1st Congressional District in Wisconsin just misses my home town of Whitewater. Which is good since I would not feel comfortable with him representing me in Washington if I still lived there.

I haven't heard any disparaging words about Ryan being a nazi sympathizer except for the following:

In 2012, a *top California Democrat likened Republican vice presidential candidate Paul Ryan to Nazi Joseph Goebbels. A top Kansas Democrat is likening Ryan to Adolf Hitler.*

Pat Lehman is "the dean of Kansas Democratic delegates," according to the <u>Wichita Eagle</u>. The paper reports:

Lehman said Republicans, especially vice presidential nominee Paul Ryan, are on track to "dismantle Medicare and Medicaid and every other social program, including education."

She said education is the only route most Americans can use to improve their lives and "the thought of having our public education system basically devastated, I'm really worried about that."

Lehman said her biggest concern about the election itself is voter-identification laws that Republicans have pushed through in a number of states, including Kansas.

She said the purpose is to suppress the vote, especially among Democratic-leaning constituencies such as elderly voters. And she scorned the Republicans' contention that the laws are designed to combat voter fraud.

"It's like Hitler said, if you're going to tell a lie, tell a big lie, and if you tell it often enough and say it in a loud enough

*voice, some people are going to believe
you," Lehman said.*

Read what you want, but I just think he
is a die-in-wool RINO.

3. **Sen. Marco Rubio (R-FL)**

*Republicans like McCain and Graham,
who are moderates on immigration,*

backed a comprehensive-reform agenda and saw Rubio as a potential ally. And in 2013, in what would later be cast as his central betrayal of Tea Party principles, Rubio agreed to join the bipartisan effort, which included Democrats Chuck Schumer and Robert Menendez and became known as the Gang of Eight.

Rubio's handling of the Gang of Eight negotiations might offer a window into his executive style. "He was the guy who would show up late, leave early and leave the dirty work to his staff," recalls one aide who worked behind the scenes on the bill. "You'd have a situation where all the members would be in the room and a couple of senators would be arguing, and then Rubio's staffer would be arguing, while Rubio would be sitting back with a Cheshire-cat grin on his face, watching."

Rubio listens to Senator John McCain speak about the crisis in Syria, in 2011. Alex Wong/Getty

To the shock of many people who were involved with the bill, Rubio outsourced the bulk of the negotiations to a close friend and hired gun, Miami attorney Enrique Gonzalez. While hiring experts is far from unusual, Gonzalez is an attorney at one of the most prominent corporate immigration law firms in the country, and Rubio made him the head of his team. "Enrique's role was to make sure the business community loved this bill and knew who it was who took care of them," says the aide. "From a political standpoint, that was a smart play. But it was also incredibly irresponsible, a case study in the donor class controlling our politics. And what it says about what kind of president Rubio would be is quite frightening." This is why Trump's attacks on Rubio have resonated — "He's right," the staffer continues. "The establishment looks at him and says, 'He'll play ball.' And the immigration bill is evidence of that."

But few saw this aspect of Rubio's work. Instead, he almost immediately became the face of immigration reform, upstaging established reform advocates in his party like Graham and McCain, who several people say resented the young senator's star power. On the other hand, "everyone knew they needed Rubio because he was their connection to the Tea Party," says the aide. "If he walked away, it would have killed the bill."

But Rubio was careful to hedge, even as he went out selling the bill to Rush Limbaugh and others in the conservative media. "Rubio would go on these shows and say things that were inaccurate," says the aide. According to some staffers, McCain would blow up at this – in one argument, an aide recalls other Republicans complaining that Rubio "spoke another language" than what he spoke to them. Later, at a press conference, Rubio tried to make a joke about it. "He was like, 'I changed my mind!' – there was almost something Hamlet-like about it all."

Unsurprisingly, the conservatives weren't convinced – later, in one epic putdown, Ann Coulter called the freshman senator "Chuck Schumer's press secretary." Rubio, seeing his support among conservatives slipping, backed away from the bill, and though it passed in the Senate, it was never even brought to the House. Immigration-reform advocates were crushed. "I have a special cold, dark place in my heart for Marco Rubio," says Sharry of America's Voice. "This guy threw immigration under the bus. Instead of pushing Republicans to embrace it, he enables them to block it. I've been around politicians for 30 years, and I know they have to lean and pander, but to see him argue for immigration reform in June 2013, and then argue with equal conviction against it a few months later, that is really disturbing."

4. Gov. John Kasich, (R-OH)

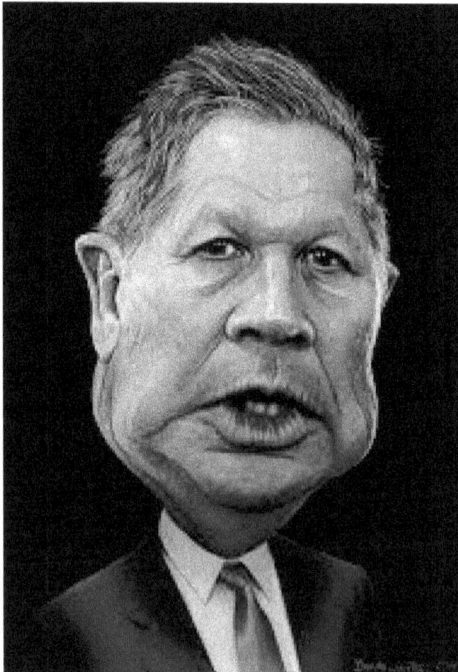

Ohio Gov. John Kasich said during a joint CNN town hall Tuesday with Vermont Sen. Bernard Sanders that his instincts were right about President Trump.
Mr. Kasich, who unsuccessfully ran against Mr. Trump in last year's Republican presidential primary, said the allegations that Mr. Trump shared Israeli intelligence about the Middle East with the Russians is "a very, very serious matter."

"I don't like people that say, 'I told you so,' but you both know how much pressure, criticism and heat I took because I was the one Republican who would not endorse Donald Trump," he told CNN's Dana Bash and Jake Tapper.

"The things that have swirled around this White House are the reasons that caused me not to move forward and support him," he added. "Part of my

concern was not just some of what I saw during that campaign, but also there wasn't a real grasp on the issues that I think are so important."

John is still sore about losing to the Donald that he couldn't say anything nice if he had honey dripping from his lips.

5. Sen Lindsey Graham (R-SC)

Lindsey is a close RINO with John McCain. They both seem to like to speak badly about President Trump no matter what he does.

Picking a first among equals when it comes to hating on Trump is no easy task, but the South Carolina senator stands out for two main reasons: His willingness to speak out publicly and how he does so with such flair. "You'll never convince me that Donald Trump is the answer to the problem we have with Hispanics,

" Graham said in March. "It will tear the party apart, it will divide conservatism, and we're gonna lose to Hillary Clinton and have the third term of Barack Obama." Back in January Graham said that "if you nominate Trump and Cruz, I think you get the same outcome," he

told reporters. "Whether it's death by being shot or poisoning doesn't really matter. I don't think the outcome will be substantially different." (He eventually endorsed Cruz.) On the day Trump won the Indiana primary effectively sealed the GOP nomination, Graham tweeted this:

Follow

Lindsey Graham
✔

@LindseyGrahamSC
If we nominate Trump, we will get destroyed.......and we will deserve it.
2:03 PM - 3 May 2016

When you have Republicans like this, either they need to change parties or we do.   AND I don't mean go over to the Democrat Party.

6. Rep Carlos Curbelo (R-FL).

One of the most vulnerable Republicans in Congress, Florida Rep. Carlos Curbelo, is so intent on getting credit for being the first GOP lawmaker to discuss impeaching President Donald Trump that his office called up Mother Jones magazine and got them add a correction to a recent story.

"Following publication, a spokeswoman for Curbelo contacted Mother Jones to point out that Congressman Curbelo was actually the first Republican to mention impeachment,'" reads the correction.

The article originally stated that Michigan Rep. Justin Amash, a libertarian who often breaks with his party, was the first. Neither congressman has advocated impeaching Trump, but both have noted publicly it is a possible outcome of Trump's firing of former FBI Director James Comey.

Curbelo could be a bellwether for further defections in the House GOP ranks. His Miami-area congressional district — which was recently profiled by NBC News — last year voted for Hillary Clinton by a larger margin than the districts of any of his GOP colleagues on the ballot in 2018, making Curbelo a top target for Democrats.

The sophomore lawmaker had a tough reelection fight last year, and made a point of declaring publicly that he would not vote for Trump.

Curbelo has lately been more visible than normal in local and national media to discuss the controversies engulfing the Trump White House.

I'm not calling any of the above, Nazis. BUT, they are displaying Nazi tendencies and act like Nazis that you just have to judge for yourself.

My hatred toward Nazism goes back to my childhood. When I was about five, a neighbor wrote a swastica on our front window with soap on Halloween. My mother was mortified and scrubbed it off as soon as she could.

We are of German origin and we even belonged to the Lutheran Church, which was called the German Lutheran Church, because every 5th Sunday the sermon would be in German. During the war, the FBI even came to listen to a sermon to determine if anything was subversive.

We found out that the young person that defiled our window had an even bigger hatred toward the Nazis. His older brother was killed on a mission over Germany. We could excuse his soaping and let his parents know that we were not sympathizers with the Nazis and were terribly sorry for their loss.

The Nazis were/are very much like the radical Islam terrorists today. They killed who ever they wanted and felt no remorse or sorrow to the family and friends of those they killed. They have to be the most hated band of terrorists just like ISIS is today. No one can possible sleep peacefully at night doing the terrible atrocities they have committed.   ISIS believes they will receive their reward when they die, but it won't be heaven.   The Nazis believed that Adolf was their Jesus and killing was sanctioned.

Liberals, today, also believe they are doing the right thing, but burning, looting and in the cases of accidental or suicidal deaths in the Democratic Party is the same thing that the Nazis were doing. How this Clinton crime family has gone on this long is testament to how corrupted things are in Washington.

The people of Germany, during the war, also were anesthetized to the travesty that was going on and didn't raise a finger to stop it.   If fact they came to believe that it was probably OK since the Führer wanted it.

The chief liberals are like the Führer in that what they say goes.   The sheep will follow those that tell the biggest lies and talk the loudest.

What's wrong with America? People think these people are political experts!

These are some of the "expert" liberals that want to lead you to the promised land. Each one is all mouth. BUT, they believe they are in an unique position in life to be able to tell you what to do.

Most just have to much money and not enough brains. They are unable to carry out what they tell the rest of us to do. They are very much like Adolf. All mouth and brains that fail them when they need it the most.

Fake News

A sign of our times - fake news has become prevalent and the stations that are accused of it don't seem to care.

It's no secret that most of the news agencies are liberal in their writings and broadcasting. They seem to have been bought off to slant all their news reporting in the liberal vein. Those that still speak the conservative word seem to be losing their standing.

It's a terrible blight on America's reputation of calling a spade a spade. The lies that are being told to our citizens are so blatant that most can see the errors immediately. Those that we previously trusted for the truth have been found out to be paid to slant their murmurings. We need the old type reporters that dug for the truth and reported their findings. The Watergate reporting was the last of the best.

Maybe some of the blame belongs to the college professors, who seem to fall into the liberal category and who teach our young minds the socialistic way of life. You would think that if they truly believed in all their socialistic rhetoric they would teach for free. After all - income equality and sharing are a great part of the propaganda shoved out at all the leftist rallies.

I am truly fearful that our youth are being "Hitlerized" by our own education system. It even goes down into the high school and grade school level. Some of the subjects being taught are directly in opposition to our countries values.

We cannot make America great again with this subterfuge going on. The media has to tell the TRUTH. We can live with that. They won't hurt our feelings. Those that preach the lies and substitute it for the truth are devils looking to destroy our country.

Reflecting

In my nearly 80 years, I have lived through 13 Presidents starting with the 2nd term of Roosevelt and ending with Obama. Most seemed to excel at their job with a few exceptions:

Franklin Roosevelt was a needed President to try and get us out of a bad recession. However, his work programs didn't do that well until WWII. Many believe that he knew as much about December 7th, 1941 as the Japanese.

Harry Truman was the last Democrat I ever had hope in. His ability to make the BIG decisions and taking responsibility for them was impressive. He also believed that you can't become wealthy by being a good politician.

Dwight Eisenhower was my Commander-in-Chief during my tour in the Air Force. I believe he was the most qualified in that position since Washington.

John Kennedy - Although he was more humanistic he was still very political. He also was a mentor to Clinton as a womanizer. He was cut short in his efforts to help this country.

Lyndon Johnson was a big blow hard. He was all talk and started the country on the downward spiral. He was cunning and devious as well as a womanizer.

Richard Nixon was a master at foreign relations, but terrible on the domestic front. He fell apart doing what seems to be common place now in Washington. He did the right thing by resigning.

Gerald Ford was a good fill in for Nixon. A gentle man who stumbled through life, but always had a smile. He tried hard.

Jimmie Carter took the prize as being the worst President up until that time. He felt he was always right and the times and circumstances proved him wrong. He was weak responding to threats and acts against our nation.

Ronald Reagan was a breath of fresh air. Regained love for our country and fired back at those that meant it harm. Someone you could look up to and be proud.

George H. W. Bush started off where Reagan left off, but went off the path at the end of his term. He was one of the first modern day New World Order (NWO) believers which didn't seem like much then until the truth started to come out.

William Clinton Bill always had a sneaky air about him. He wanted you to believe him, but many didn't. He talked a good fight, but never really followed through. He became only the second President to be impeached by the House of Representatives. His womanizing topped them all. AND - the champion still reigns.

George W. Bush His Presidency was marked by 9-11 and his entire eight years was based around it. He sought revenge against threats to his father after the first Iraqi war. This started the spiral of wars against terrorism. Patriotic to say the least.

Barack Hussain Obama without a doubt the leader as the worst President in history. Surrounded himself with

Islamic eccentrics and lied his way into a 2nd term. The damage to our country is incalculable and will take years to undue. Cozied up to terrorist countries and allowed their operatives to enter our country. Disrespected our allies, troops and police. Always took the side of the Blacks regardless of who was at fault. He will NOT be missed.

Epilogue

What must we do to correct all the wrongs that have been perpetrated on our country?

- Eliminate our enormous debt or at least reduce it significantly. This will be hard since those that like to spend money still have a loud voice.
- Eliminate corruption in Washington and State governments. This, again, will be hard since it has become a way of life. Those that receive bribes have become used to it and expect it.

- Get rid of voter complacency. We have representatives serving now that have no idea of how to do it except to talk loud and long. The more they talk the more of an idiot they become.
- Reduce the size of the government. The government has become the problem and not the solution. The cost of government is way to high. This is another reason that corruption is rampant.
- Keep those that mean to do us harm out of the country. Whether that means we build a wall in the south increase our surveillance in the west, east and north - it must be done. Things just won't get better by doing nothing.
- Deport illegal immigrants, especially those that are already in prison or have been convicted of other crimes besides being illegal. This is not a dumping ground for other countries bad people.

- Quit challenging the Constitution. It has served us well for over 240 years and is NOT in need of updating.
- Stop those that riot, burn and destroy by putting them in jail. No one has the right to destroy another's property.
- Reduce spending on food stamps and benefits for the professional moochers. If they have four wives and 10 kids, they need a JOB.
- Take care of our veterans. They deserve care before any refugee or illegal.
- Lower taxes and reduce regulations so the economy can grow.
- Get rid of both the Republican and Democrat Parties and start a Liberal and Conservative movement. We already have conservative Democrats and liberal Republicans. Lets truly distinguish each representative.
- Send liars and leakers to jail.
- Regulate the media so *fake news* can be punishable. Outright lying in the media is wrong and needs to stop.

- Law breakers, politicians, CEO's, bankers or whoever should be judged by the same laws as the normal law breaker. NO ONE IS ABOVE THE LAW.
- Politicians making the laws should be required to live by the law.
- All members of Congress should be held to term limits. Representatives - 12 years (6 terms) and Senators to 16 years (2 terms). Their retirement monies should also be scaled way back. These are not life long occupations.
- Keep the Electoral College for voting in Presidential elections, but require ID for every voter.
- Put prayer back in schools.
- Forbid any Muslim sharia court system. We already have a court system and don't need a special one.
- Those that disrespect the flag should be punished.
- Those that leave the country to join a recognized terror group should lose their citizenship.

Many more suggestions could be added, but one of the first things that need to be done is to divest ourselves of the Nazi mentality that is so prevalent in our country. People in supervisory capacity, such as teachers, should not try and supplement their political ideas on the students. Young minds are like sponges and soak up everything coming their way. Liberals have more of the Nazi mentality than any other group.

Our courts need to be adjusted to adjudicate the law and not try to establish their feelings of the law. Anyone threatening the safety of the country or our citizens needs to be dealt with quickly and thoroughly.

May God Bless our Country AGAIN

Thanks for listening. *Ron*

Finally - Again

I can't help but say a few words about the condition of our country before this book goes to press. Times change quickly and so do the people who are liberal.

I don't believe there has ever been a more unsettling time in our country than the last eight plus years. We watched as the country slowly went southward and turned from a patriotic nation into a sheep filled one led by a ravenous fox who had nothing but hate and contempt for our beloved nation. He promised everything, but delivered on nothing. The younger minds believed all his lies and voted for him in great numbers.

It wasn't just the younger people who voted for him, but even learned people who fell for his dangling carrot. People like Senator Ted Kennedy from

Massachusetts who proclaimed BO as the next savior for our nation. It's really to bad that he died before he could see the damage that BO caused. I'm sure that President John Kennedy would have had trouble backing BO if he would have still been alive.

Now that the progressives have their eight solid years at the feed trough, they are very unwilling to give it up and help turn our country around to what it was originally designed for.

During the months leading up to the 2016 Presidential election, their one candidate was assured to be the winner. How they thought that was, simple - rig the election just like the previous election or two happened.

BUT - this time the "other" side had a candidate that the progressives couldn't really put their finger on and overcome. He was a non-politician, wealthy self-made man who wasn't indebted to no one and had more money than the bribers had. He did things differently and the voting public came to him in droves. He basically financed his campaign and even flew his own airplane. He was met by thousands wherever he landed.

This man won the election and the progressives cried foul. They said they had more popular votes and he only won the electoral college votes. Needless to say that if you take all the illegal votes away from the progressives he won both the popular and electoral votes. Now the liberals are crying foul and started looting, burning and berating the winner because they realized that their free meal ticket was just cancelled.

Now, even well passed his "100 free days" President Trump is besieged by liberals, as well as Republicans, who want to bring him down. He has done more good in his first 100 days than BO did in EIGHT YEARS. This man is destined to become a VERY GOOD PRESIDENT - IF NOT THE BEST.

Some of the dumbest carbon life forms on this planet are in the US Government

Hank Johnson
Thinks the island of Guam will tip over if overpopulated

Sheila Jackson Lee
Thinks the US Constitution is 400 years old

Hank finds being a mouth-breathing moron an effortless challenge

Sheila makes no excuse for being completely vacuous

Maxine Waters
Thinks Putin invaded Korea

Nancy Pelosi
Said we have to pass the (Obamacare) bill so that you can find out what is in it

The stupidity is strong with this one, Maxine is the epitome of an ignoramus

Pelosi clearly has the highest IQ in the Demorrhoid party at an impressive 50

This is what brain dead looks like

Trying to bring him down are some of the dumbest representatives this country has ever known.   AND - somehow they keep getting re-elected.

The losing candidate in 2016 has finally recovered to the point that she now is proclaiming she is part of the "resistance". She isn't any smarter than the dumbos pictured above.

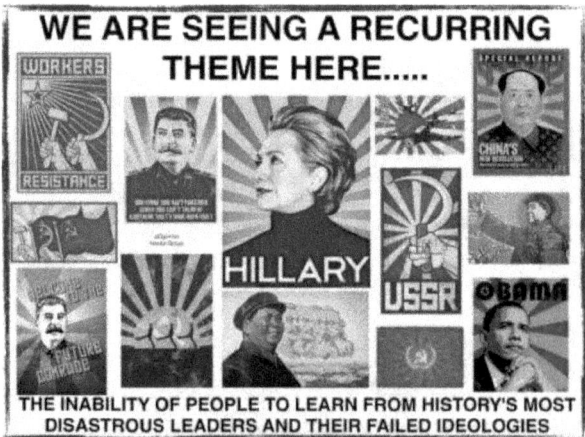

WE ARE SEEING A RECURRING THEME HERE.....

HILLARY

THE INABILITY OF PEOPLE TO LEARN FROM HISTORY'S MOST DISASTROUS LEADERS AND THEIR FAILED IDEOLOGIES

Finally - The End

Every Honest, Red
Blooded American
owes President Donald
John Trump a BIG
debt of Gratitude for
taking on this thankless
Job.

www.ingramcontent.com/pod-product-compliance
Lightning Source LLC
Chambersburg PA
CBHW060509030426
42337CB00015B/1806